THE SKELETAL SYSTEM

Text: Eduard Arnau
Illustrations: Antonio Muñoz Tenllado

Nuestra arquitectura ósea © Copyright Parramón Ediciones, S.A.
Published by Parramón Ediciones, S.A.,
Barcelona, Spain.

The Skeletal System copyright © 1995 by Chelsea House
Publishers, a division of Main Line Book Co.
All rights reserved.

1 3 5 7 9 8 6 4 2

Nuestra arquitectura ósea. English.
   The skeletal system.
      p. cm. — (Invisible world)
   Includes index.
   ISBN 0-7910-3151-9
   1. Human skeleton—Juvenile literature.
[1. Skeleton.] I. Chelsea House Publishers. II. Title.
III. Series.
QM101. N8413 1995   94-28303
611'.71—dc20   CIP
                                                          AC

Contents

INVISIBLE WORLD

THE SKELETAL SYSTEM

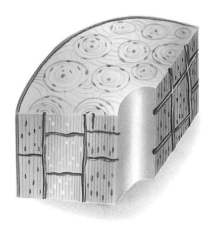

CHELSEA HOUSE PUBLISHERS

New York • Philadelphia

A Multifunctional System

The skeleton, a rigid structure created from approximately 206 bones, forms the basis of the body's shape and external appearance, including its height. This strong, resistant frame protects the most important bodily organs, such as the heart, the lungs, the brain, and the spinal cord.

The skeleton acts as a base for movement, with its rigidity permitting the bones to support the body's weight despite gravity's downward pull. These sturdy bones work with the rest of the locomotive apparatus—the joints, structures that link the bones together, and more than 400 muscles—to allow us a range of motion.

The bone system has other, less obvious but no less crucial functions. The bone marrow at the center of bones manufactures the cells of the blood: red blood cells, white blood cells, and platelets. These cells play a vital role in keeping the body healthy. The bone system also stores a deposit of diverse nutrients and minerals, particularly calcium, that are essential for the correct development and functioning of the body.

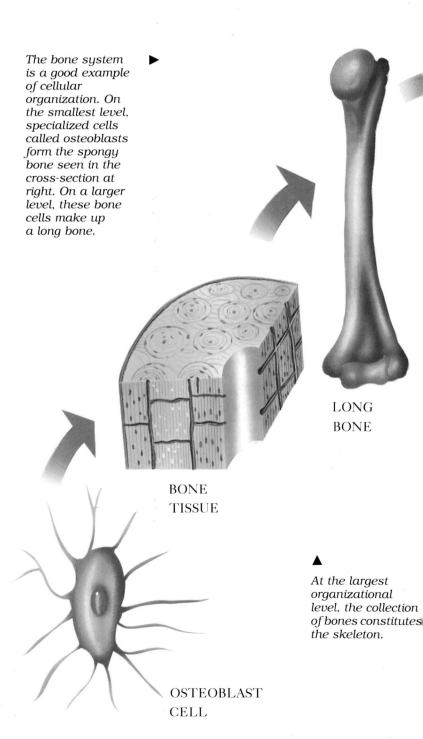

The bone system is a good example of cellular organization. On the smallest level, specialized cells called osteoblasts form the spongy bone seen in the cross-section at right. On a larger level, these bone cells make up a long bone.

LONG BONE

BONE TISSUE

▲

At the largest organizational level, the collection of bones constitutes the skeleton.

OSTEOBLAST CELL

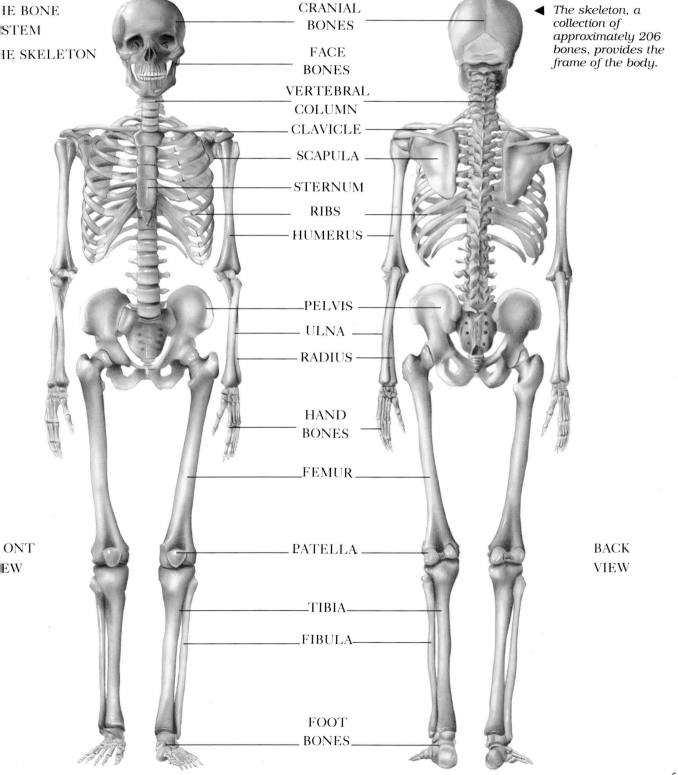

THE BONE
STEM

HE SKELETON

CRANIAL
BONES

FACE
BONES

VERTEBRAL
COLUMN

CLAVICLE

SCAPULA

STERNUM

RIBS

HUMERUS

PELVIS

ULNA

RADIUS

HAND
BONES

FEMUR

PATELLA

TIBIA

FIBULA

FOOT
BONES

The skeleton, a collection of approximately 206 bones, provides the frame of the body.

ONT
EW

BACK
VIEW

Bone Composition

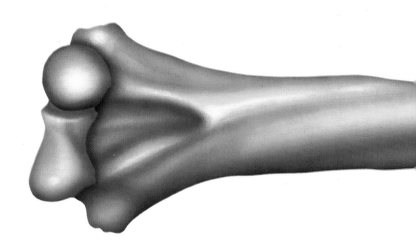

Bones are divided into three basic parts. First, they are enclosed by the periosteum, fibrous tissue that contains numerous blood vessels to nourish the bone. The periosteum covers the whole surface except for areas where cartilage connects the bone to a joint.

Underneath the periosteum lie layers of hard, dense bone and hollow ducts known as Haversian canals, which carry nerves and blood vessels. Lacunae, small holes in the bone, contain osteocytes, cells that store and release calcium. This compact bone can act as a protective layer to spongy bone, which provides support against the forces on the ends of a bone.

Inside spongy bone is the medullary tissue or bone marrow. Red bone marrow produces red blood cells, white blood cells, and platelets. Yellow marrow stores fat, providing a reserve energy source when body fat has been reduced.

Newborns possess only red bone marrow, but during the growth phase, part of it converts into yellow medullary tissue. If you become anemic, with an extremely low supply of red blood cells, yellow marrow can be transformed into red marrow to fill the need.

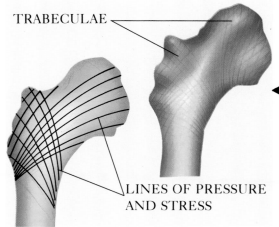

TRABECULAE

LINES OF PRESSURE AND STRESS

◀ *Bones are expertly engineered to resist pressure and stress. Trabeculae spikelike structures in spongy bone, add support against the forces acting on the epiphyses, or ends of the bones.*

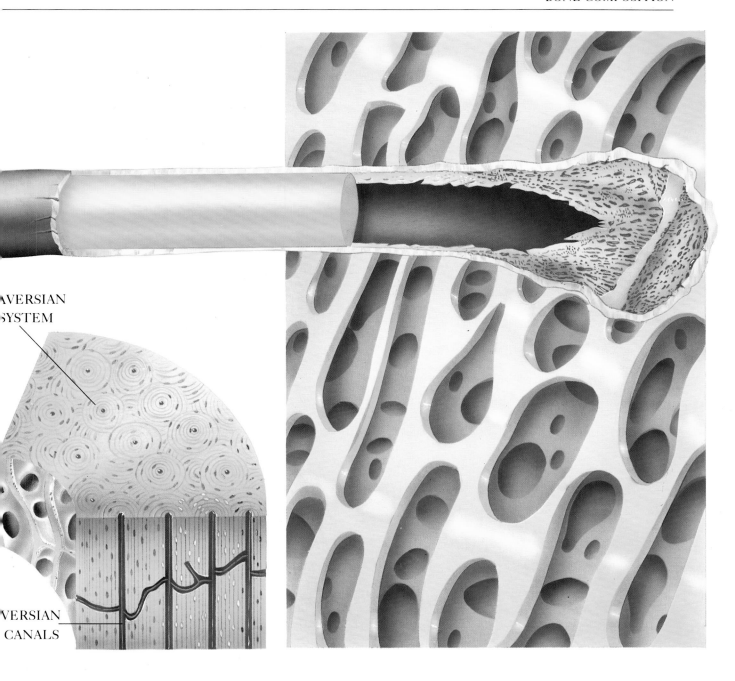

HAVERSIAN
SYSTEM

HAVERSIAN
CANALS

Long bones such as the humerus in the arm produce blood cells in the red bone marrow, which fills the many cavities of the spongy bone tissue (1) in the epiphyses. Compact bone (2) tissue gives the bone its strength. The diaphysis or center of the bone consists of yellow bone marrow (3), which stores fat. The bone is covered by a kind of skin or covering called the periosteum (4).

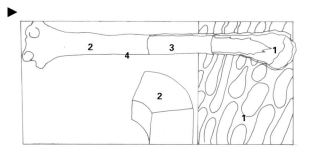

Red Blood Cell Production

Red bone marrow, found in the central part of short and flat bones and in the ends of long ones, acts as a veritable factory for red blood cells, also known as erythrocytes. Two hundred billion new cells are created each day, replacing the erythrocytes that wear out after four months and are disintegrated by the spleen and liver.

Twenty-five trillion red blood cells are swept through the bloodstream, making up nearly 45 percent of the solid portion of the blood. The only body cells to lack a nucleus, erythrocytes are narrow disks elastic enough to squeeze through the tiniest capillaries.

Red blood cells perform a duty that is absolutely crucial to life: the delivery of oxygen to all the body's cells. The erythrocytes' hemoglobin, an iron compound that gives the blood its red tint, attaches to oxygen in the lungs and then releases it to each cell as the red blood cells circulate through the capillaries.

During cellular respiration, cells require oxygen to transform nutrients into the energy the body needs to carry out its diverse functions. Hemoglobin passes oxygen into the cells and collects carbon dioxide, the waste product of respiration, to return to the lungs.

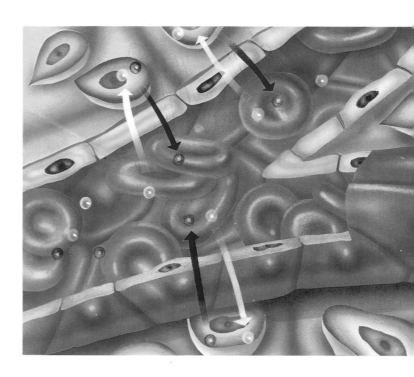

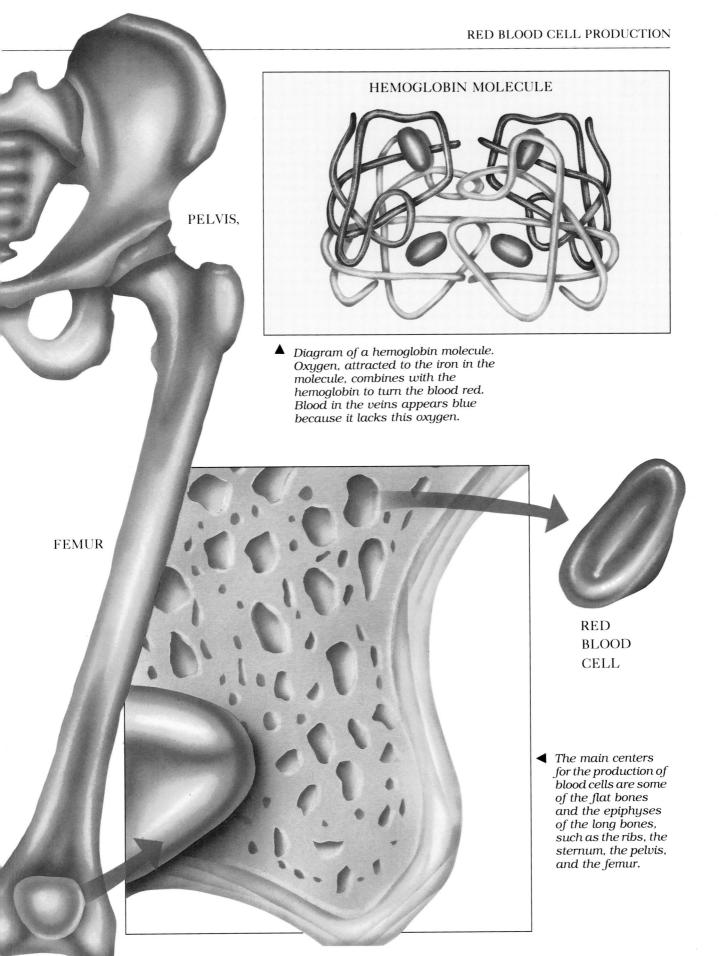

HEMOGLOBIN MOLECULE

PELVIS,

▲ *Diagram of a hemoglobin molecule. Oxygen, attracted to the iron in the molecule, combines with the hemoglobin to turn the blood red. Blood in the veins appears blue because it lacks this oxygen.*

FEMUR

RED
BLOOD
CELL

◄ *The main centers for the production of blood cells are some of the flat bones and the epiphyses of the long bones, such as the ribs, the sternum, the pelvis, and the femur.*

The Defensive Function

White blood cells, or leukocytes, also originate in red bone marrow, although a variety called lymphocytes are produced by the lymph glands. A healthy person has between 7 and 10 million white blood cells in each cubic inch of blood.

White blood cells have the important function of defending the body from infection. Whenever the body is in danger of illness, more leukocytes are manufactured. Though bigger than red blood cells, white blood cells can still move through capillary and cell walls to reach the area under attack from harmful germs.

The immune system responds in a few different ways to bacterial and viral assaults. When such antigens are detected, proteins called antibodies are produced. Antibodies counteract the damaging effect of antigens by dividing or clumping them together to be attacked by more white cells. Some antibodies can neutralize the antigens by attaching themselves to the foreign material. Once the body has been exposed to a particular antigen, it develops specific antibodies to deal with it, making you more resistant to that disease.

White blood cells called phagocytes kill germs and decaying cells by surrounding and then eating them. Some leukocytes, which normally survive around two weeks, perish while fighting hostile organisms. The thick pus which forms from some infections contains these dead leukocytes and bacteria, as well as some living white blood cells. Other leukocytes assist in healing the body by becoming scar-tissue cells.

Platelets, small oval cells created in the red bone marrow and lymph nodes, maintain the body's health by forming clots to keep all the blood from flowing out of wounds. When they encounter a torn blood vessel, platelets disintegrate and combine with a thread-like substance called fibrin to create a scab.

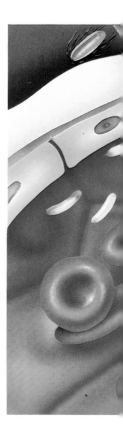

The body's line of defense. When a blood vessel is broken (1), platelets adhere to its wall and coagulate the blood. Meanwhile, white blood cells (2) consume the bacteria (3) which have entered the wound.

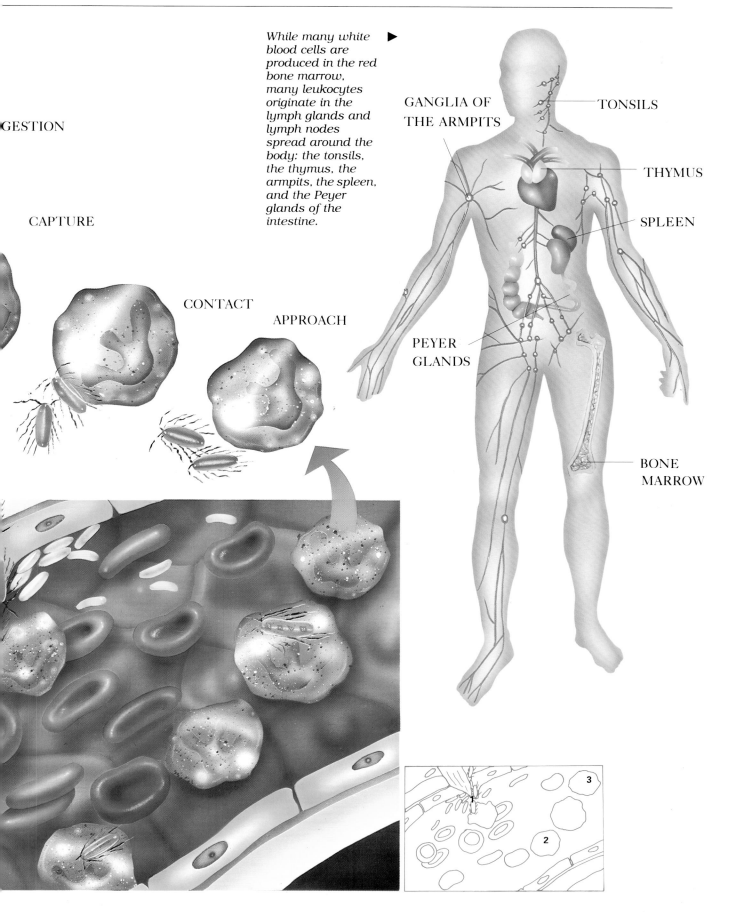

While many white blood cells are produced in the red bone marrow, many leukocytes originate in the lymph glands and lymph nodes spread around the body: the tonsils, the thymus, the armpits, the spleen, and the Peyer glands of the intestine. ▶

GESTION

CAPTURE

CONTACT

APPROACH

GANGLIA OF
THE ARMPITS

TONSILS

THYMUS

SPLEEN

PEYER
GLANDS

BONE
MARROW

Bones and Height

Although bones begin developing during the fetal period, at birth they are not completely calcified, particularly at their ends or epiphyses. Ossification, or hardening, occurs as specialized cells known as osteoblasts produce spongy bone to replace the more flexible cartilage.

During childhood and adolescence, the epiphyseal plates in the bones determine growth. The cartilage in the growth plate lengthens, forming successive layers of bone tissue on the extremities of the bone. Total ossification of the cartilage—and the end of growth—occurs between the ages of 20 and 25. However, bones may continue to expand in diameter as they gain in strength.

This entire process is regulated by genetic and hormonal factors, with the pituitary, thyroid, and parathyroid glands as well as the ovaries (female sex organs) and testes (male sex organs) all contributing. The pituitary, which secretes the human growth hormone, plays an especially crucial part.

Once bones are formed, they can take five very different shapes, depending on their function. Long bones, found in the arms and legs, have a thin central shaft, or diaphysis, and two epiphyses to support the body's weight. Short bones like the carpal in the wrist, nearly cube-shaped with equal length and width, possess much strength but little mobility. Irregular bones like the vertebrae have many dimensions similar to short bones but appear in a range of shapes adapted to their role. Flat bones, such as the broad, thin bones in the ribs, protect the body's delicate internal organs. Finally, sesamoidal bones, small and round, are found in the part of a tendon that is compressed during movement, such as the patella in the knee.

SESAMOIDAL BONE
PATELLA

Examples of the five ▶
different bone
shapes.

LONG BONE
FEMUR

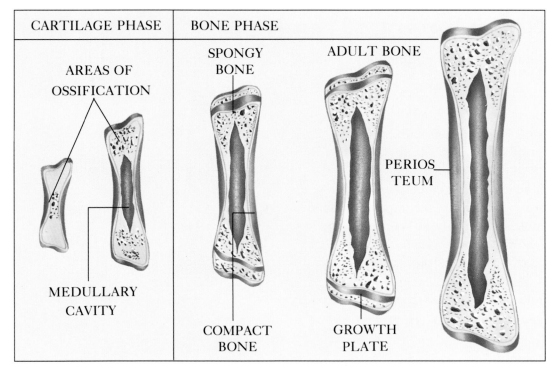

CARTILAGE PHASE	BONE PHASE

AREAS OF OSSIFICATION

MEDULLARY CAVITY

SPONGY BONE

COMPACT BONE

ADULT BONE

GROWTH PLATE

PERIOS_ TEUM

The bones lengthen ▶ as layers of cartilage are replaced by hard bone tissue. Growth ends by the age of 25.

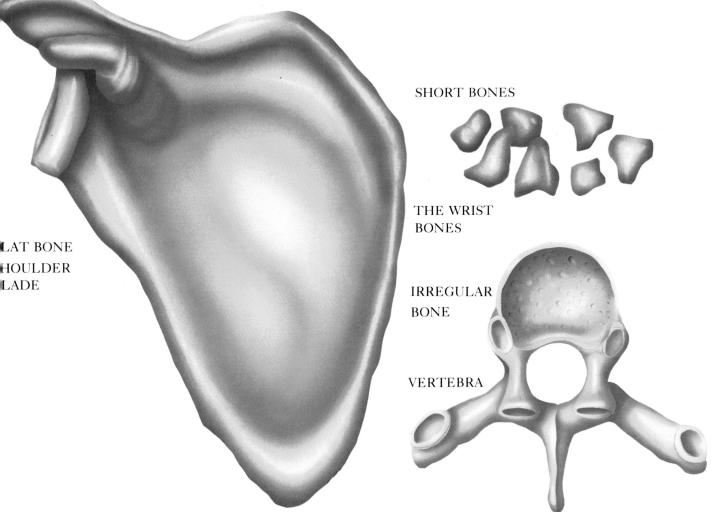

FLAT BONE
SHOULDER BLADE

SHORT BONES

THE WRIST BONES

IRREGULAR BONE

VERTEBRA

Nourishment of the Bone

In a constant cycle of formation and destruction, the bone is a living organ, with blood vessels and its own metabolism that interact with the rest of the body. One of the minerals the body needs is calcium, which affects blood clotting, nerve impulses, and muscle contractions. When calcium levels in the blood fall, bone cells called osteoclasts break down some of the material between the bone cells (the bone matrix) to release calcium into the bloodstream.

When the blood carries an excess of calcium, osteocytes absorb and store the calcium. Osteocytes, mature bone cells, are the basis of bone tissue that give the bone its hardness and fragility. The rest of the tissue consists of organic matter such as collagen, which gives the bone elasticity.

The development and strengthening of the bone depends on vitamin D and vitamin D2 or calciferol, which regulates the absorption of calcium and phosphate in the intestine. Milk, eggs, and codfish are good sources of vitamin D; a well-balanced diet should provide you with all the vitamins and nutrients you need. Moderate exposure to the sun's ultraviolet rays improves the absorption of vitamin D.

Bones are also strengthened by exercise, because force on the bones encourages more collagen fibers and inorganic minerals to be deposited in the bone matrix. Thus, exercise combined with a calcium-rich diet will prevent osteoporosis, the progressive decalcification of bones that increases the risk of fractures.

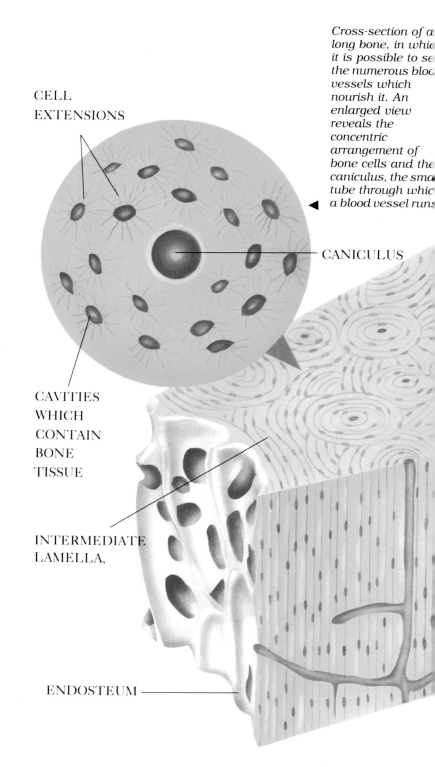

CELL EXTENSIONS

Cross-section of a long bone, in which it is possible to see the numerous blood vessels which nourish it. An enlarged view reveals the concentric arrangement of bone cells and the caniculus, the small tube through which a blood vessel runs

CANICULUS

CAVITIES WHICH CONTAIN BONE TISSUE

INTERMEDIATE LAMELLA,

ENDOSTEUM

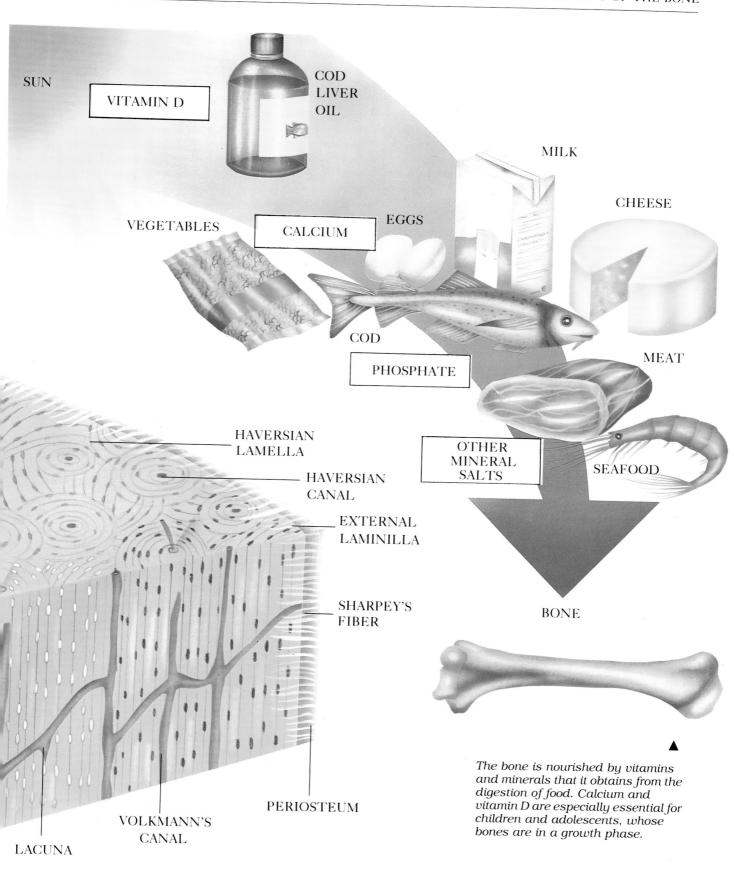

SUN

VITAMIN D

COD
LIVER
OIL

MILK

CHEESE

VEGETABLES

CALCIUM

EGGS

COD

PHOSPHATE

MEAT

HAVERSIAN
LAMELLA

HAVERSIAN
CANAL

OTHER
MINERAL
SALTS

SEAFOOD

EXTERNAL
LAMINILLA

SHARPEY'S
FIBER

BONE

PERIOSTEUM

VOLKMANN'S
CANAL

LACUNA

The bone is nourished by vitamins and minerals that it obtains from the digestion of food. Calcium and vitamin D are especially essential for children and adolescents, whose bones are in a growth phase.

The Task of Movement

Bodily movement is based on the principle of a lever. The bone is the lever itself, while the joint is the fulcrum on which the lever pivots and the muscle is the source of force. The ability to transform muscle strength into movement depends on the shape and layout of the bones. The extremities are the most representative of this locomotive function.

At the upper part of the thorax, the shoulder is made up of the collarbone (clavicle) and the shoulder blade (scapula), with a ball-and-socket joint that allows a wide range of motions. The upper arm consists of the humerus, the long bone whose lower epiphysis forms the elbow, the joint for the lower arm. The lower arm contains two bones which run parallel to each other: the ulna and the radius. These bones cross to achieve the rotation of the wrist. The wrist, hand, and fingers have a total of 27 small bones, divided into the carpals, metacarpals, and phalanges.

The lower limbs begin at the pelvis or pelvic girdle, which is wider and more angled in women to assist the passage of the fetus during birth. The thigh is composed of the femur, the longest bone in the human body. The kneecap, also called the patella, is a small, round, flat bone that assists the leg in flexing and extending. Next come the tibia (shinbone) and the fibula, which resemble the ulna and radius. The ankle and foot are made up of 26 bones arranged in three groups: the ankle bones (tarsals), metatarsals, and phalanges. The metatarsals and phalanges are similar to the bones in the hands but are less well-developed.

The toes, which have joints like the fingers but are not as mobile, help us keep our balance. The calcaneus in the heel, the biggest bone in the foot, absorbs shocks and acts as a cushion against the jolts which occur with every step.

▼

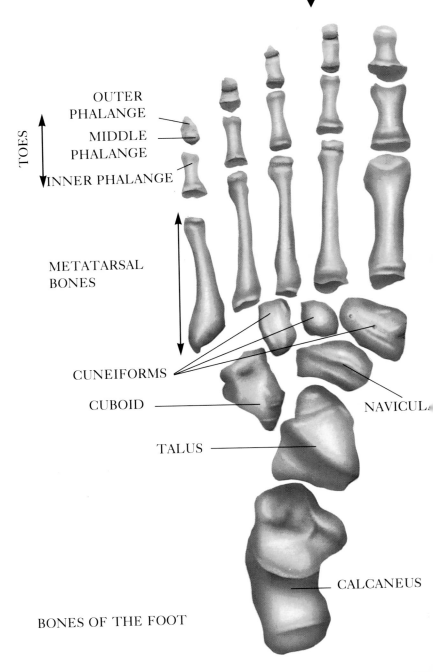

TOES

OUTER PHALANGE

MIDDLE PHALANGE

INNER PHALANGE

METATARSAL BONES

CUNEIFORMS

CUBOID

NAVICUL

TALUS

CALCANEUS

BONES OF THE FOOT

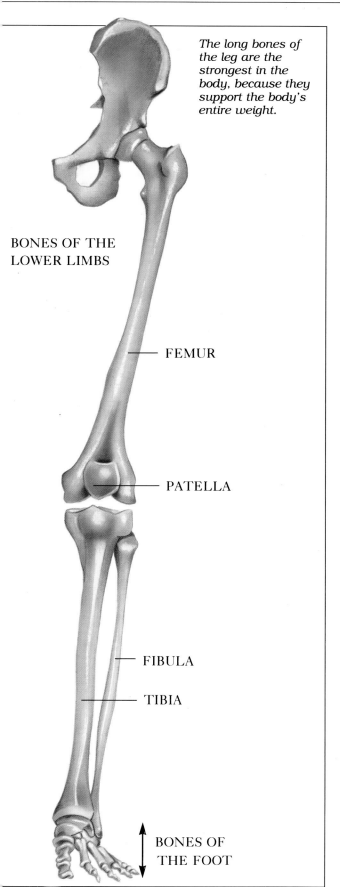

The long bones of the leg are the strongest in the body, because they support the body's entire weight.

BONES OF THE
LOWER LIMBS

FEMUR

PATELLA

FIBULA

TIBIA

BONES OF
THE FOOT

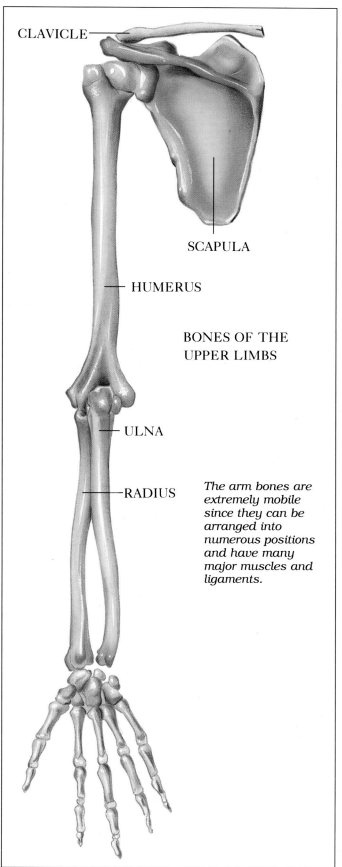

CLAVICLE

SCAPULA

HUMERUS

BONES OF THE
UPPER LIMBS

ULNA

RADIUS

The arm bones are extremely mobile since they can be arranged into numerous positions and have many major muscles and ligaments.

Joints, Specialized Parts of the Locomotive System

Synovial joints, the only kind that can move freely, come in all shapes and sizes to allow a variety of movements. For example, the humerus and the ulna meet at the elbow in a hinge joint, which permits movement in only one direction. On the other hand, the ball-and-socket joints in the shoulders and hips, in which a bone with a round end fits into a bone with a round groove, allow many different actions. Condylar joints like those in the knees are similar to ball-and-socket joints but have ligaments that prevent full rotation. A saddle joint between two saddle-shaped bone epiphyses, such as at the base of the thumb, also fosters an array of motions.

Joints facilitate the smooth movement of certain parts of the skeleton while keeping others solidly united. The synovial membrane covers the internal surface of the joint and secretes synovial fluid to lubricate the cartilage and nourish it, since the joints lack blood vessels. Resilient cartilage tissue acts as a cushion for the epiphyses, easing the friction caused by the continual rubbing between the bones and absorbing the shocks from high-impact movements. Ligaments, bands of tough, fibrous tissue, firmly connect the bones to each other in the joint and limit the extent of their movements.

The different structures of joints determine which movements are possible. The ball-and-socket joint allows the widest range of motion.

▼

TYPES OF JOINTS

HINGE

BALL-AND-SOCKET

ARTHRODIAL

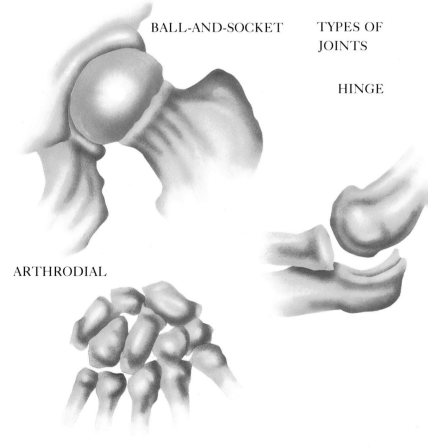

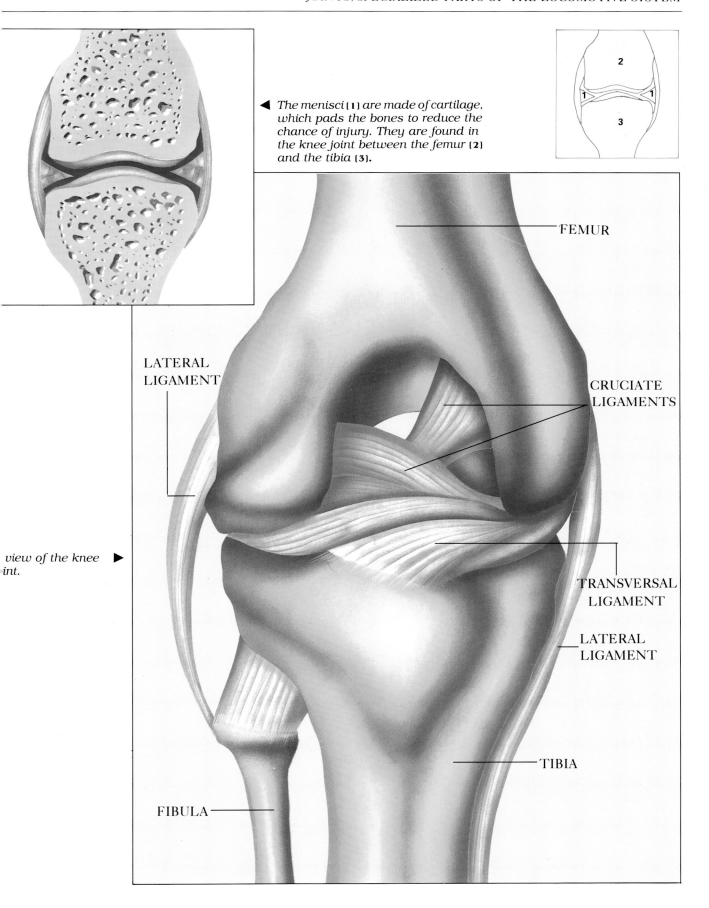

◄ *The menisci* (**1**) *are made of cartilage, which pads the bones to reduce the chance of injury. They are found in the knee joint between the femur* (**2**) *and the tibia* (**3**).

FEMUR

LATERAL
LIGAMENT

CRUCIATE
LIGAMENTS

view of the knee ►
int.

TRANSVERSAL
LIGAMENT

LATERAL
LIGAMENT

TIBIA

FIBULA

Skull and Face Bones

The head bones are divided into two parts: the posterior or skull, which protects the brain, and the anterior or face, which houses most of the sense organs and supports the mastication apparatus.

The skull is composed of eight flat, very strong bones linked by fixed joints:

— The two parietal bones are found in the upper lateral (side) areas.
— The two temporal bones are located in the lower part and protect the hearing and balance organs.
— The frontal bone forms the forehead, acts as a base for the skull, and contains two deep cavities or orbits for the eyeballs.
— The occipital bone is positioned in the lower, posterior part of the skull. It has a large, internal orifice, the foramen magnum, which links the skull with the spinal cord in the vertebral column and through which the main nerve canals pass.
— The ethmoid is a small bone which comprises part of the external wall of the nasal passages.
— The sphenoid in the center, front part of the skull's base shelters the pituitary gland.

The bones of the face are divided into two areas or mandibles. The upper mandible is formed by two fixed bones, the upper maxillaries, and the lower one by an articulated joint, the lower maxillary bone, whose main function is chewing.

The joints between the bones in the skull and face are fixed, providing support but no movement. In the skull, they form a zig-zagging line called a suture, which offers extra-solid protection, while in the face, they are linked in a straight line.

▼

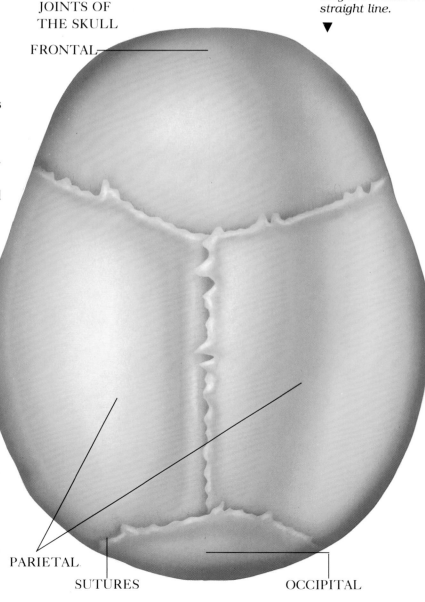

JOINTS OF THE SKULL

FRONTAL

PARIETAL

SUTURES

OCCIPITAL

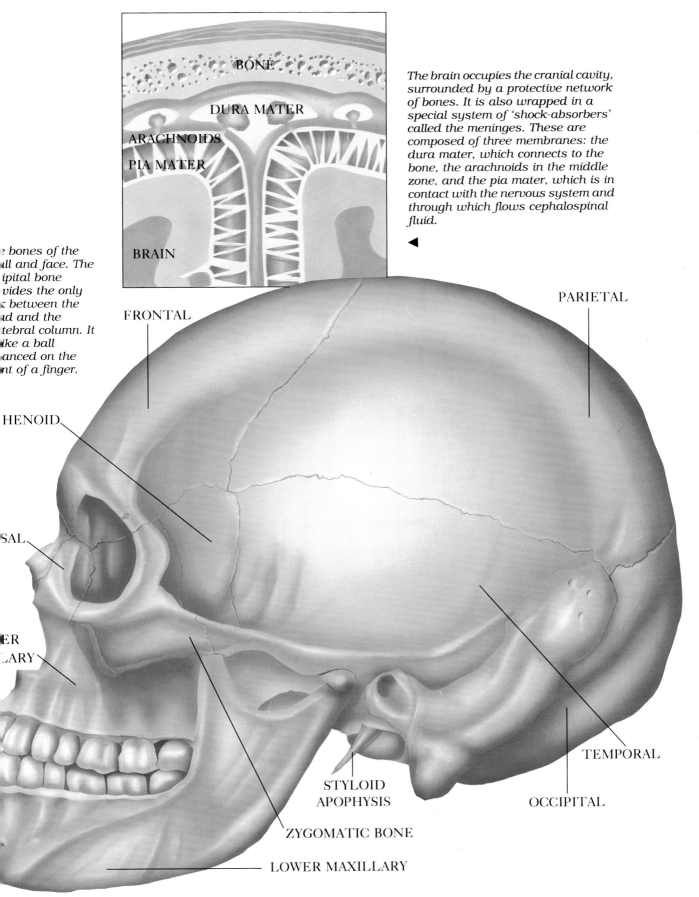

BONE

DURA MATER

ARACHNOIDS

PIA MATER

BRAIN

The brain occupies the cranial cavity, surrounded by a protective network of bones. It is also wrapped in a special system of 'shock-absorbers' called the meninges. These are composed of three membranes: the dura mater, which connects to the bone, the arachnoids in the middle zone, and the pia mater, which is in contact with the nervous system and through which flows cephalospinal fluid.

◄

e bones of the
ll and face. The
ipital bone
vides the only
between the
d and the
tebral column. It
ke a ball
anced on the
nt of a finger.

HENOID

SAL

ER
LARY

PARIETAL

FRONTAL

TEMPORAL

OCCIPITAL

STYLOID
APOPHYSIS

ZYGOMATIC BONE

LOWER MAXILLARY

The Vertebral Column, Protection for the Spinal Cor

The vertebral column is the axis or main support of our body. The 33 or 34 vertebrae, placed in line one above the other, together make up the spinal canal, which houses the spinal cord. Each vertebra has a central hole plus various small protuberances, the apophyses, to which the muscles are attached.

The vertebrae are distributed in the following way:

— 7 cervical: these are the least thick and the most mobile. The first cervical vertebra, the atlas, is an incomplete vertebra. The second, the axis, allows the lateral rotation of the neck.
— 12 dorsal: these correspond to the area of the upper back and are thicker and less mobile than the cervical vertebrae.
— 5 lumbar: these reasonably mobile vertebrae are found in the area of the waist.

— 5 sacral: these are welded together to form the sacrum, a strong bone which acts as the base of the vertebral column.
— 4 or 5 coccygeal: these are also strongly joined together, to form the coccyx (tail bone).

The fragile spinal cord is very well protected, surrounded by spinal fluid and guarded by the sturdy vertebrae. It serves the important function of providing the main pathway for messages in the central nervous system, which stretches from the brain to the lumbar vertebrae. Along the spinal cord's nerve fibers, sensory nerves relay stimuli to the brain, and motor neurons transmit the brain's orders to the body's muscles.

Vertebrae are irregular bones filled with spongy tissue. Their shape varies according to their place in the spinal column.

▼

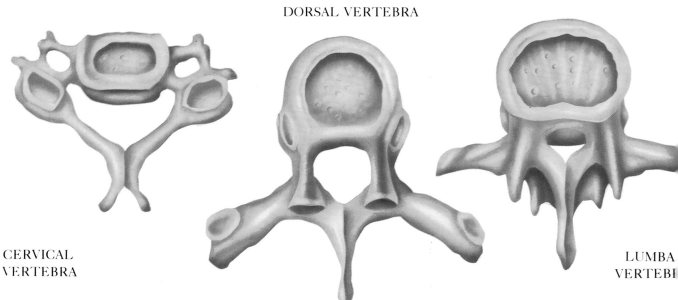

DORSAL VERTEBRA

CERVICAL
VERTEBRA

LUMBA
VERTEBF

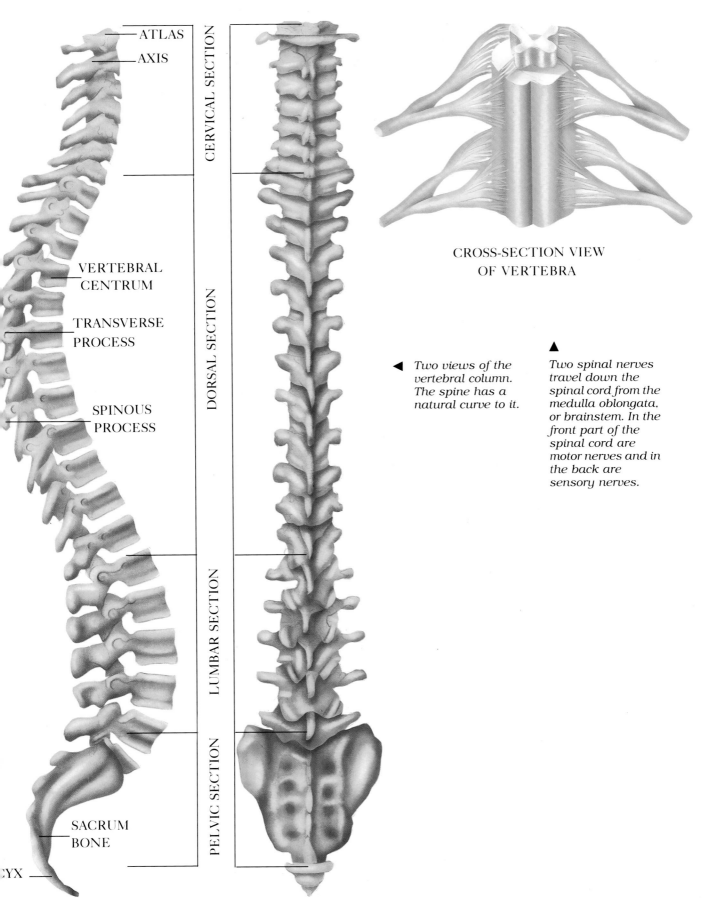

ATLAS

AXIS

VERTEBRAL
CENTRUM

TRANSVERSE
PROCESS

SPINOUS
PROCESS

SACRUM
BONE

CYX

CERVICAL SECTION

DORSAL SECTION

LUMBAR SECTION

PELVIC SECTION

CROSS-SECTION VIEW
OF VERTEBRA

◄ *Two views of the vertebral column. The spine has a natural curve to it.*

▲
Two spinal nerves travel down the spinal cord from the medulla oblongata, or brainstem. In the front part of the spinal cord are motor nerves and in the back are sensory nerves.

The Thorax, Protector of the Lungs and Heart

The thorax, the upper part of the torso, houses the lungs and the heart. The thoracic cage, constructed of the ribs and sternum, shelters these vital organs.

The ribs are formed of 24 long, thin bones joined at the back to the spinal column. The first seven pairs are called true ribs, because each is connected by cartilage to the sternum. The remaining five pairs are known as false ribs, because they are not linked directly to the sternum but are all joined together by their respective cartilages. The so-called floating ribs, the eleventh and twelfth pairs, are not attached in the front at all.

The sternum or breastbone is the broad, flat bone located at the front of the thorax. About six inches long, it is joined to the two clavicles of the shoulders and to the seven true ribs.

The thoracic cage plays a fundamental part in the respiratory mechanism. At the bottom of the thoracic cavity lies an umbrella-shaped muscle, the diaphragm. When the diaphragm contracts, it pushes up the ribs, increasing the volume of the thoracic cage and allowing us to inhale. During exhalation, the ribs are pulled down by the abdominal obliques.

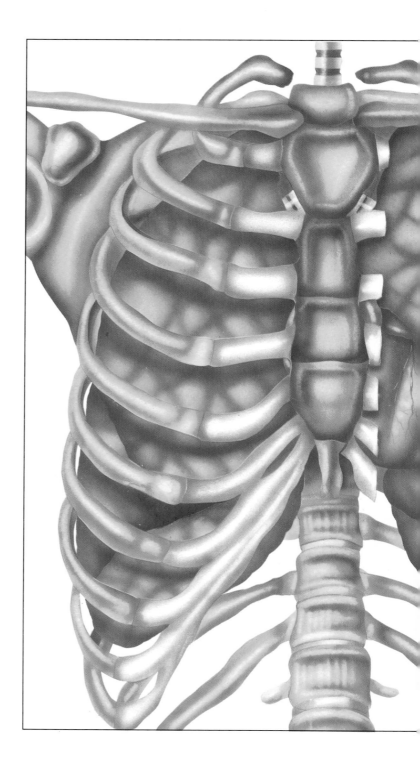

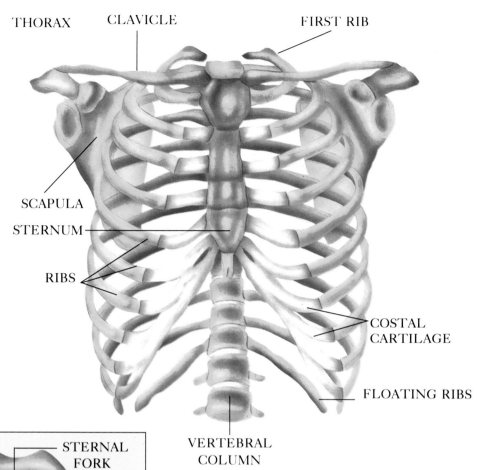

THORAX

CLAVICLE

FIRST RIB

SCAPULA

STERNUM

RIBS

COSTAL CARTILAGE

FLOATING RIBS

VERTEBRAL COLUMN

◄ *The thoracic cage, which keeps the heart and lungs safe, is involved in movements key to breathing. Muscles expand the cage to permit the intake of air and then return it to its original dimensions to force air from the lungs.*

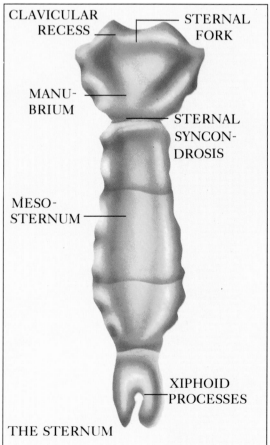

CLAVICULAR RECESS

STERNAL FORK

MANU-BRIUM

STERNAL SYNCON-DROSIS

MESO-STERNUM

XIPHOID PROCESSES

THE STERNUM

◄ *The sternum or breastbone, a flat bone. Its upper part, or manubrium, is the widest, and its central part has a series of recesses for the ribs.*

▲ *The thorax is delineated by the sternum, the ribs, and the vertebral column. The ribs, flat bones in the shape of an arc, are connected to the dorsal vertebrae at the back.*

Fractures and Dislocations

Although the elements of the locomotive apparatus are quite strong and flexible, sudden, excessive twisting or compression on the bone can cause an injury.

A fracture occurs when a bone breaks, either wholly or partially. In the most serious type, a compound fracture, the injured bone breaks through the skin, exposing the body to infection. Any fractured bone must be realigned and immobilized by a cast or a splint. Healing time depends on a person's age, because over time, osteoblasts become less efficient at producing new bone—it takes eight weeks for an adult's collarbone to mend, compared to two weeks for a newborn.

When the ends of the two bones in a joint move out of their normal position, usually because of a direct blow, a dislocation results. After the joint has been relocated, it may have to be immobilized.

The unnatural twisting of a joint may stretch or tear the surrounding ligaments, causing a sprain. A minor sprain can usually be treated with rest, ice, and supportive bandages.

The regeneration process of a fractured bone is one of the most beautiful demonstrations of the body's ability repair itself. These are the principal stages:

1. Broken blood vessels form clots and white blood cells fight any infection.

1

2

3

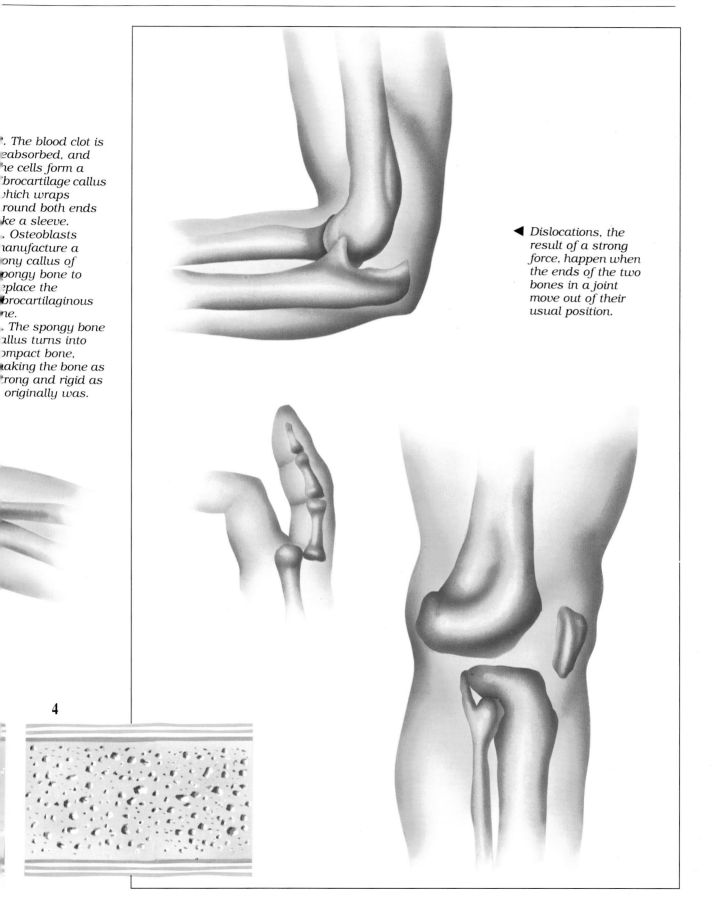

. The blood clot is
reabsorbed, and
the cells form a
fibrocartilage callus
which wraps
around both ends
like a sleeve.
. Osteoblasts
manufacture a
bony callus of
spongy bone to
replace the
fibrocartilaginous
one.
. The spongy bone
callus turns into
compact bone,
making the bone as
strong and rigid as
it originally was.

◀ Dislocations, the
result of a strong
force, happen when
the ends of the two
bones in a joint
move out of their
usual position.

4

Look and Learn

CHICKEN BONE

GLASS JAR,

VINEGAR

Height: What time is it?

The next time someone asks you how tall you are, tell her that it depends what time it is. To prove that this isn't a joke, find a tape measure, a pencil, and some paper.

As soon as you get up in the morning, stand with your back against a wall, your feet together, and your eyes looking straight ahead. Have someone measure your height, and note it down on the sheet of paper. Just before you go to bed at night, do it again. Now how tall are you? Repeat the measurement for several days in a row. What do you notice?

The bones in the vertebral column are separated by disks of soft tissue, which absorb shocks. During the day gravity pulls the vertebral column downward, and the pressure causes the disks to lose water—so when you go to bed, you are slightly shorter than when you got up. During the night the disks regain the water.

Bend a Bone

When we are born, our bones are relatively soft, since they have a lot of cartilage in them. As we grow, our bones become harder, especially the outer part, thanks to deposits of minerals such as calcium and phosphate.

You can observe the opposite process of bones changing from hard to soft. Find a chicken's thigh bone, a glass jar, and some vinegar. Clean any traces of meat from the bone, put it in the jar, and pour vinegar over it until it is covered. After a few days, renew the vinegar, and repeat the process for three or four weeks. Then take the bone out of the jar and dry it. It will bend as if it was made of rubber. If it is long enough you will even be able to tie it in a knot. This is possible because the vinegar has dissolved most of the hard minerals which make up the bone; without them the bone is like the cartilage of the nose or the earlobe.

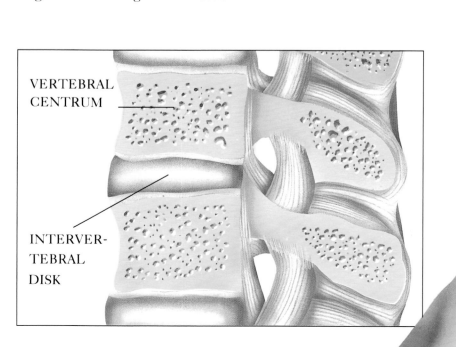

VERTEBRAL CENTRUM

INTERVER-TEBRAL DISK

Make a Sling

Fractures of the shoulder, arm, or elbow usually require a sling. You can practice how to make one with a friend so that perhaps one day, if it is necessary, you will be able to help someone who has suffered this type of accident.

You can improvise a sling using a large scarf, as in the illustration. Hold the arm in the fold of the scarf and tie the ends behind the neck or the damaged shoulder.

It is also possible to stop a fractured arm or leg from getting worse by using a splint. This can be made from a rolled-up newspaper or a piece of wood and tied on using a scarf or a belt. The most important thing is that the splint is long enough to cover the broken bone and the neighboring joints.

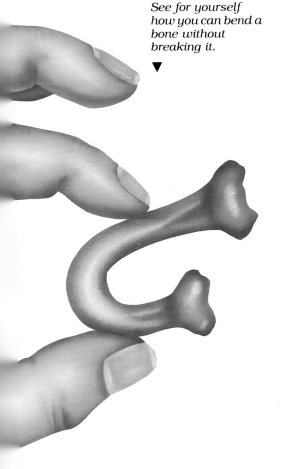

See for yourself how you can bend a bone without breaking it. ▼

The damaged arm is held still by using a folded scarf tied behind the neck or the shoulder.

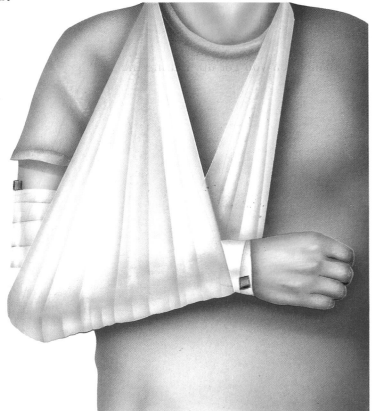

29

GLOSSARY

antibody *a protein manufactured by the body to fight bacteria, viruses, and other foreign substances*

antigen *a foreign substance which antibodies attack*

cartilage *a tough, resilient connective tissue that cushions bones in the joints*

compact bone *dense bone that gives strength to the diaphysis and covers spongy bone*

diaphragm *the umbrella-shaped muscle used in breathing, located just below the lungs*

diaphysis *the shaft of a long bone*

dislocation *an injury in which the bones in a joint are dislodged from their proper position*

epiphysis *the end of a long bone*

erythrocyte *a red blood cell, which delivers oxygen to the cells*

fracture *an injury in which a bone breaks*

growth plate *a section of cartilage between the epiphysis and diaphysis that allows the bone to lengthen*

Haversian canal *duct that carries blood vessels and nerves through the bone*

hemoglobin *an iron compound that attaches to oxygen and gives red blood cells their color*

leukocyte *a name for white blood cells, which fight infection*

ligament *fibrous tissue that connects the bones in a joint*

matrix *material found between bone cells, where calcium is stored*

meninges *the three membranes which surround and protect the brain and spinal cord*

ossification *hardening of the bones*

osteoblast *a cell that forms bone matrix*

osteoclast *a cell that removes excess bone*

osteocyte *a mature bone cell that stores and releases calcium*

osteoporosis *a disease that involves the decalcification and weakening of bones; it primarily affects older women*

periosteum *the external covering of a bone*

phagocyte *white blood cell that devours germs*

platelet *a cell that clots blood*

red bone marrow *medullary tissue which produces blood cells*

spleen *a small organ near the stomach that destroys old red blood cells*

spongy bone *bone which has beamlike structures for support and many marrow-filled cavities*

sprain *an injury in which the ligaments connecting the bones in a joint are stretched or torn*

suture *immovable joint where the bones of the skull meet*

tendon *connective tissue between muscle and bone*

yellow bone marrow *medullary tissue which stores fat*

NDEX

Real Life, Real Progress
for Children with
Autism Spectrum Disorders